50 Sweet and Savory Pancake Recipes

By: Kelly Johnson

Table of Contents

- Classic Buttermilk Pancakes
- Banana and Walnut Pancakes
- Blueberry Lemon Pancakes
- Chocolate Chip Pancakes
- Pumpkin Spice Pancakes
- Cinnamon Roll Pancakes
- Strawberry Shortcake Pancakes
- Peanut Butter Banana Pancakes
- Maple Bacon Pancakes
- Nutella and Strawberry Pancakes
- Matcha Green Tea Pancakes
- Lemon Ricotta Pancakes
- Almond Joy Pancakes (Coconut, Almonds, Chocolate)
- S'mores Pancakes
- Coconut Pancakes with Pineapple
- Red Velvet Pancakes
- Savory Cheddar and Chive Pancakes
- Spinach and Feta Pancakes
- Kimchi Pancakes
- Zucchini and Corn Pancakes
- Chicken and Waffles Pancakes
- Savory Potato and Chive Pancakes
- Mediterranean Feta and Olive Pancakes
- Thai-Style Savory Pancakes
- Herb and Goat Cheese Pancakes
- Sweet Potato Pancakes with Maple Syrup
- Peach Cobbler Pancakes
- Savory Mushroom and Thyme Pancakes
- Apple Cinnamon Pancakes
- Bacon and Cheddar Pancakes
- Raspberry Lemonade Pancakes
- Savory Carrot and Onion Pancakes
- Chocolate Banana Pancakes
- Tomato and Basil Pancakes
- Blackberry Sage Pancakes

- Savory Beetroot Pancakes
- Honey Lavender Pancakes
- Jalapeño Cornbread Pancakes
- Coconut Lime Pancakes
- Feta and Spinach Pancakes
- Chocolate Mint Pancakes
- Corn and Zucchini Pancakes
- Blackberry Coconut Pancakes
- Herb and Parmesan Pancakes
- Honey Almond Pancakes
- Savory Egg and Cheese Pancakes
- Churro Pancakes
- Savory Quinoa and Spinach Pancakes
- Maple Pecan Pancakes
- Sweet and Savory Vegetable Pancakes

Classic Buttermilk Pancakes

Ingredients:

- 1 cup all-purpose flour
- 2 tablespoons sugar
- 1 teaspoon baking powder
- 1/2 teaspoon baking soda
- 1/4 teaspoon salt
- 1 cup buttermilk
- 1 large egg
- 2 tablespoons melted butter
- Oil or butter for frying

Instructions:

1. In a bowl, mix flour, sugar, baking powder, baking soda, and salt.
2. In another bowl, whisk together buttermilk, egg, and melted butter.
3. Combine wet and dry ingredients until just mixed.
4. Heat oil or butter in a skillet over medium heat.
5. Pour batter onto the skillet and cook until bubbles form, then flip and cook until golden brown.

Banana and Walnut Pancakes

Ingredients:

- 1 cup all-purpose flour
- 2 tablespoons sugar
- 1 teaspoon baking powder
- 1/2 teaspoon baking soda
- 1/4 teaspoon salt
- 1 ripe banana (mashed)
- 1 cup buttermilk
- 1 large egg
- 1/4 cup chopped walnuts
- Oil or butter for frying

Instructions:

1. In a bowl, mix flour, sugar, baking powder, baking soda, and salt.
2. In another bowl, combine mashed banana, buttermilk, and egg.
3. Mix wet and dry ingredients, then fold in walnuts.
4. Heat oil or butter in a skillet over medium heat.
5. Pour batter onto the skillet and cook until bubbles form, then flip and cook until golden brown.

Blueberry Lemon Pancakes

Ingredients:

- 1 cup all-purpose flour
- 2 tablespoons sugar
- 1 teaspoon baking powder
- 1/2 teaspoon baking soda
- 1/4 teaspoon salt
- 1 cup buttermilk
- 1 large egg
- Zest of 1 lemon
- 1/2 cup fresh blueberries
- Oil or butter for frying

Instructions:

1. In a bowl, mix flour, sugar, baking powder, baking soda, and salt.
2. In another bowl, whisk together buttermilk, egg, and lemon zest.
3. Combine wet and dry ingredients, then fold in blueberries.
4. Heat oil or butter in a skillet over medium heat.
5. Pour batter onto the skillet and cook until bubbles form, then flip and cook until golden brown.

Chocolate Chip Pancakes

Ingredients:

- 1 cup all-purpose flour
- 2 tablespoons sugar
- 1 teaspoon baking powder
- 1/2 teaspoon baking soda
- 1/4 teaspoon salt
- 1 cup buttermilk
- 1 large egg
- 1/2 cup chocolate chips
- Oil or butter for frying

Instructions:

1. In a bowl, mix flour, sugar, baking powder, baking soda, and salt.
2. In another bowl, whisk together buttermilk and egg.
3. Combine wet and dry ingredients, then fold in chocolate chips.
4. Heat oil or butter in a skillet over medium heat.
5. Pour batter onto the skillet and cook until bubbles form, then flip and cook until golden brown.

Pumpkin Spice Pancakes

Ingredients:

- 1 cup all-purpose flour
- 2 tablespoons sugar
- 1 teaspoon baking powder
- 1/2 teaspoon baking soda
- 1/4 teaspoon salt
- 1 teaspoon pumpkin pie spice
- 1 cup buttermilk
- 1 large egg
- 1/2 cup pumpkin puree
- Oil or butter for frying

Instructions:

1. In a bowl, mix flour, sugar, baking powder, baking soda, salt, and pumpkin pie spice.
2. In another bowl, whisk together buttermilk, egg, and pumpkin puree.
3. Combine wet and dry ingredients until just mixed.
4. Heat oil or butter in a skillet over medium heat.
5. Pour batter onto the skillet and cook until bubbles form, then flip and cook until golden brown.

Cinnamon Roll Pancakes

Ingredients:

- 1 cup all-purpose flour
- 2 tablespoons sugar
- 1 teaspoon baking powder
- 1/2 teaspoon baking soda
- 1/4 teaspoon salt
- 1 cup buttermilk
- 1 large egg
- 1/4 cup melted butter
- 2 tablespoons cinnamon sugar (cinnamon mixed with sugar)
- Oil or butter for frying

Instructions:

1. In a bowl, mix flour, sugar, baking powder, baking soda, and salt.
2. In another bowl, whisk together buttermilk, egg, and melted butter.
3. Combine wet and dry ingredients until just mixed.
4. Heat oil or butter in a skillet over medium heat.
5. Pour batter onto the skillet, sprinkle with cinnamon sugar, then pour a little more batter on top.
6. Cook until bubbles form, then flip and cook until golden brown.

Strawberry Shortcake Pancakes

Ingredients:

- 1 cup all-purpose flour
- 2 tablespoons sugar
- 1 teaspoon baking powder
- 1/2 teaspoon baking soda
- 1/4 teaspoon salt
- 1 cup buttermilk
- 1 large egg
- 1/2 cup sliced strawberries
- Whipped cream for topping
- Oil or butter for frying

Instructions:

1. In a bowl, mix flour, sugar, baking powder, baking soda, and salt.
2. In another bowl, whisk together buttermilk and egg.
3. Combine wet and dry ingredients, then fold in sliced strawberries.
4. Heat oil or butter in a skillet over medium heat.
5. Pour batter onto the skillet and cook until bubbles form, then flip and cook until golden brown.
6. Serve with whipped cream on top.

Peanut Butter Banana Pancakes

Ingredients:

- 1 cup all-purpose flour
- 2 tablespoons sugar
- 1 teaspoon baking powder
- 1/2 teaspoon baking soda
- 1/4 teaspoon salt
- 1 cup buttermilk
- 1 large egg
- 1/2 cup peanut butter
- 1 ripe banana (mashed)
- Oil or butter for frying

Instructions:

1. In a bowl, mix flour, sugar, baking powder, baking soda, and salt.
2. In another bowl, combine buttermilk, egg, peanut butter, and mashed banana.
3. Mix wet and dry ingredients until just combined.
4. Heat oil or butter in a skillet over medium heat.
5. Pour batter onto the skillet and cook until bubbles form, then flip and cook until golden brown.

Maple Bacon Pancakes

Ingredients:

- 1 cup all-purpose flour
- 2 tablespoons sugar
- 1 teaspoon baking powder
- 1/2 teaspoon baking soda
- 1/4 teaspoon salt
- 1 cup buttermilk
- 1 large egg
- 1/4 cup maple syrup
- 1/2 cup cooked and crumbled bacon
- Oil or butter for frying

Instructions:

1. In a bowl, mix flour, sugar, baking powder, baking soda, and salt.
2. In another bowl, whisk together buttermilk, egg, and maple syrup.
3. Combine wet and dry ingredients until just mixed.
4. Fold in crumbled bacon.
5. Heat oil or butter in a skillet over medium heat.
6. Pour batter onto the skillet and cook until bubbles form, then flip and cook until golden brown.

Nutella and Strawberry Pancakes

Ingredients:

- 1 cup all-purpose flour
- 2 tablespoons sugar
- 1 teaspoon baking powder
- 1/2 teaspoon baking soda
- 1/4 teaspoon salt
- 1 cup buttermilk
- 1 large egg
- 1/2 cup Nutella
- 1 cup sliced strawberries
- Oil or butter for frying

Instructions:

1. In a bowl, mix flour, sugar, baking powder, baking soda, and salt.
2. In another bowl, whisk together buttermilk and egg.
3. Combine wet and dry ingredients until just mixed.
4. Heat oil or butter in a skillet over medium heat.
5. Pour batter onto the skillet and add a spoonful of Nutella in the center.
6. Cook until bubbles form, then flip and cook until golden brown.
7. Serve topped with fresh strawberries.

Matcha Green Tea Pancakes

Ingredients:

- 1 cup all-purpose flour
- 2 tablespoons sugar
- 1 teaspoon baking powder
- 1/2 teaspoon baking soda
- 1/4 teaspoon salt
- 1 tablespoon matcha powder
- 1 cup buttermilk
- 1 large egg
- Oil or butter for frying

Instructions:

1. In a bowl, mix flour, sugar, baking powder, baking soda, salt, and matcha powder.
2. In another bowl, whisk together buttermilk and egg.
3. Combine wet and dry ingredients until just mixed.
4. Heat oil or butter in a skillet over medium heat.
5. Pour batter onto the skillet and cook until bubbles form, then flip and cook until golden brown.

Lemon Ricotta Pancakes

Ingredients:

- 1 cup all-purpose flour
- 2 tablespoons sugar
- 1 teaspoon baking powder
- 1/2 teaspoon baking soda
- 1/4 teaspoon salt
- 1 cup ricotta cheese
- 1 cup buttermilk
- 2 large eggs
- Zest of 1 lemon
- Juice of 1 lemon
- Oil or butter for frying

Instructions:

1. In a bowl, mix flour, sugar, baking powder, baking soda, and salt.
2. In another bowl, combine ricotta, buttermilk, eggs, lemon zest, and lemon juice.
3. Mix wet and dry ingredients until just combined.
4. Heat oil or butter in a skillet over medium heat.
5. Pour batter onto the skillet and cook until bubbles form, then flip and cook until golden brown.

Almond Joy Pancakes (Coconut, Almonds, Chocolate)

Ingredients:

- 1 cup all-purpose flour
- 2 tablespoons sugar
- 1 teaspoon baking powder
- 1/2 teaspoon baking soda
- 1/4 teaspoon salt
- 1 cup buttermilk
- 1 large egg
- 1/4 cup shredded coconut
- 1/4 cup chopped almonds
- 1/4 cup chocolate chips
- Oil or butter for frying

Instructions:

1. In a bowl, mix flour, sugar, baking powder, baking soda, and salt.
2. In another bowl, whisk together buttermilk and egg.
3. Combine wet and dry ingredients, then fold in shredded coconut, almonds, and chocolate chips.
4. Heat oil or butter in a skillet over medium heat.
5. Pour batter onto the skillet and cook until bubbles form, then flip and cook until golden brown.

S'mores Pancakes

Ingredients:

- 1 cup all-purpose flour
- 2 tablespoons sugar
- 1 teaspoon baking powder
- 1/2 teaspoon baking soda
- 1/4 teaspoon salt
- 1 cup buttermilk
- 1 large egg
- 1/2 cup mini marshmallows
- 1/4 cup chocolate chips
- Crushed graham crackers for topping
- Oil or butter for frying

Instructions:

1. In a bowl, mix flour, sugar, baking powder, baking soda, and salt.
2. In another bowl, whisk together buttermilk and egg.
3. Combine wet and dry ingredients, then fold in mini marshmallows and chocolate chips.
4. Heat oil or butter in a skillet over medium heat.
5. Pour batter onto the skillet and cook until bubbles form, then flip and cook until golden brown.
6. Serve topped with crushed graham crackers.

Coconut Pancakes with Pineapple

Ingredients:

- 1 cup all-purpose flour
- 2 tablespoons sugar
- 1 teaspoon baking powder
- 1/2 teaspoon baking soda
- 1/4 teaspoon salt
- 1 cup coconut milk
- 1 large egg
- 1/2 cup crushed pineapple (drained)
- Oil or butter for frying

Instructions:

1. In a bowl, mix flour, sugar, baking powder, baking soda, and salt.
2. In another bowl, whisk together coconut milk and egg.
3. Combine wet and dry ingredients, then fold in crushed pineapple.
4. Heat oil or butter in a skillet over medium heat.
5. Pour batter onto the skillet and cook until bubbles form, then flip and cook until golden brown.

Red Velvet Pancakes

Ingredients:

- 1 cup all-purpose flour
- 2 tablespoons sugar
- 1 teaspoon baking powder
- 1/2 teaspoon baking soda
- 1/4 teaspoon salt
- 1 cup buttermilk
- 1 large egg
- 2 tablespoons cocoa powder
- 2 tablespoons red food coloring
- Oil or butter for frying

Instructions:

1. In a bowl, mix flour, sugar, baking powder, baking soda, salt, and cocoa powder.
2. In another bowl, whisk together buttermilk, egg, and red food coloring.
3. Combine wet and dry ingredients until just mixed.
4. Heat oil or butter in a skillet over medium heat.
5. Pour batter onto the skillet and cook until bubbles form, then flip and cook until golden brown.

Savory Cheddar and Chive Pancakes

Ingredients:

- 1 cup all-purpose flour
- 2 tablespoons baking powder
- 1/2 teaspoon baking soda
- 1/4 teaspoon salt
- 1 cup buttermilk
- 1 large egg
- 1/2 cup shredded cheddar cheese
- 1/4 cup chopped fresh chives
- Oil or butter for frying

Instructions:

1. In a bowl, mix flour, baking powder, baking soda, and salt.
2. In another bowl, whisk together buttermilk and egg.
3. Combine wet and dry ingredients, then fold in cheddar cheese and chives.
4. Heat oil or butter in a skillet over medium heat.
5. Pour batter onto the skillet and cook until bubbles form, then flip and cook until golden brown.

Spinach and Feta Pancakes

Ingredients:

- 1 cup all-purpose flour
- 1 teaspoon baking powder
- 1/2 teaspoon baking soda
- 1/4 teaspoon salt
- 1 cup buttermilk
- 1 large egg
- 1 cup fresh spinach, chopped
- 1/2 cup feta cheese, crumbled
- Oil or butter for frying

Instructions:

1. In a bowl, mix flour, baking powder, baking soda, and salt.
2. In another bowl, whisk together buttermilk and egg.
3. Combine wet and dry ingredients until just mixed.
4. Fold in chopped spinach and crumbled feta.
5. Heat oil or butter in a skillet over medium heat.
6. Pour batter onto the skillet and cook until bubbles form, then flip and cook until golden brown.

Kimchi Pancakes (Kimchi Jeon)

Ingredients:

- 1 cup all-purpose flour
- 1 cup water
- 1 cup kimchi, chopped
- 2 green onions, chopped
- 1/4 teaspoon salt
- Oil for frying

Instructions:

1. In a bowl, mix flour, water, chopped kimchi, green onions, and salt until combined.
2. Heat oil in a skillet over medium heat.
3. Pour batter into the skillet and spread it out evenly.
4. Cook until the edges are crispy and golden, then flip and cook until the other side is golden.

Zucchini and Corn Pancakes

Ingredients:

- 1 cup all-purpose flour
- 1 teaspoon baking powder
- 1/2 teaspoon baking soda
- 1/4 teaspoon salt
- 1 cup zucchini, grated and drained
- 1 cup corn kernels (fresh or canned)
- 1/2 cup buttermilk
- 1 large egg
- Oil or butter for frying

Instructions:

1. In a bowl, mix flour, baking powder, baking soda, and salt.
2. In another bowl, combine grated zucchini, corn, buttermilk, and egg.
3. Mix wet and dry ingredients until just combined.
4. Heat oil or butter in a skillet over medium heat.
5. Pour batter onto the skillet and cook until bubbles form, then flip and cook until golden brown.

Chicken and Waffles Pancakes

Ingredients:

- 1 cup all-purpose flour
- 2 tablespoons sugar
- 1 teaspoon baking powder
- 1/2 teaspoon baking soda
- 1/4 teaspoon salt
- 1 cup buttermilk
- 1 large egg
- Cooked chicken tenders
- Maple syrup for serving
- Oil or butter for frying

Instructions:

1. In a bowl, mix flour, sugar, baking powder, baking soda, and salt.
2. In another bowl, whisk together buttermilk and egg.
3. Combine wet and dry ingredients until just mixed.
4. Heat oil or butter in a skillet over medium heat.
5. Pour batter onto the skillet and cook until bubbles form.
6. Top each pancake with a chicken tender before flipping.
7. Cook until golden brown and serve with maple syrup.

Savory Potato and Chive Pancakes

Ingredients:

- 1 cup grated potatoes (about 1 medium potato)
- 1/2 cup all-purpose flour
- 1/4 teaspoon baking powder
- 1/4 teaspoon salt
- 1/4 cup chopped chives
- 1/2 cup buttermilk
- 1 large egg
- Oil or butter for frying

Instructions:

1. In a bowl, mix grated potatoes, flour, baking powder, salt, and chives.
2. In another bowl, whisk together buttermilk and egg.
3. Combine wet and dry ingredients until just mixed.
4. Heat oil or butter in a skillet over medium heat.
5. Pour batter onto the skillet and cook until crispy and golden on both sides.

Mediterranean Feta and Olive Pancakes

Ingredients:

- 1 cup all-purpose flour
- 1 teaspoon baking powder
- 1/2 teaspoon baking soda
- 1/4 teaspoon salt
- 1/2 cup feta cheese, crumbled
- 1/4 cup chopped olives (Kalamata or green)
- 1/2 cup buttermilk
- 1 large egg
- Oil or butter for frying

Instructions:

1. In a bowl, mix flour, baking powder, baking soda, and salt.
2. In another bowl, whisk together buttermilk and egg.
3. Combine wet and dry ingredients until just mixed.
4. Fold in crumbled feta and chopped olives.
5. Heat oil or butter in a skillet over medium heat.
6. Pour batter onto the skillet and cook until golden brown on both sides.

Thai-Style Savory Pancakes

Ingredients:

- 1 cup all-purpose flour
- 1 teaspoon baking powder
- 1/4 teaspoon salt
- 1/2 cup coconut milk
- 1 large egg
- 1/2 cup shredded carrots
- 1/4 cup chopped cilantro
- 1/4 cup green onions, chopped
- Chili sauce for serving
- Oil for frying

Instructions:

1. In a bowl, mix flour, baking powder, and salt.
2. In another bowl, whisk together coconut milk and egg.
3. Combine wet and dry ingredients until just mixed.
4. Fold in carrots, cilantro, and green onions.
5. Heat oil in a skillet over medium heat.
6. Pour batter onto the skillet and cook until golden brown on both sides.
7. Serve with chili sauce.

Herb and Goat Cheese Pancakes

Ingredients:

- 1 cup all-purpose flour
- 1 teaspoon baking powder
- 1/4 teaspoon salt
- 1 cup buttermilk
- 1 large egg
- 1/2 cup crumbled goat cheese
- 1/4 cup mixed fresh herbs (parsley, thyme, basil)
- Oil or butter for frying

Instructions:

1. In a bowl, mix flour, baking powder, and salt.
2. In another bowl, whisk together buttermilk and egg.
3. Combine wet and dry ingredients until just mixed.
4. Fold in crumbled goat cheese and herbs.
5. Heat oil or butter in a skillet over medium heat.
6. Pour batter onto the skillet and cook until golden brown on both sides.

Sweet Potato Pancakes with Maple Syrup

Ingredients:

- 1 cup all-purpose flour
- 1/2 teaspoon baking powder
- 1/2 teaspoon baking soda
- 1/4 teaspoon salt
- 1 cup cooked and mashed sweet potato
- 1 cup buttermilk
- 1 large egg
- Maple syrup for serving
- Oil or butter for frying

Instructions:

1. In a bowl, mix flour, baking powder, baking soda, and salt.
2. In another bowl, combine mashed sweet potato, buttermilk, and egg.
3. Mix wet and dry ingredients until just combined.
4. Heat oil or butter in a skillet over medium heat.
5. Pour batter onto the skillet and cook until bubbles form, then flip and cook until golden brown.
6. Serve with maple syrup.

Peach Cobbler Pancakes

Ingredients:

- 1 cup all-purpose flour
- 1 tablespoon sugar
- 1 teaspoon baking powder
- 1/2 teaspoon baking soda
- 1/4 teaspoon salt
- 1 cup buttermilk
- 1 large egg
- 1 cup peaches, diced (fresh or canned)
- 1 teaspoon cinnamon
- Maple syrup for serving
- Butter for frying

Instructions:

1. In a bowl, mix flour, sugar, baking powder, baking soda, salt, and cinnamon.
2. In another bowl, whisk together buttermilk and egg.
3. Combine wet and dry ingredients until just mixed, then fold in diced peaches.
4. Heat butter in a skillet over medium heat.
5. Pour batter onto the skillet and cook until bubbles form, then flip and cook until golden brown.
6. Serve with maple syrup.

Savory Mushroom and Thyme Pancakes

Ingredients:

- 1 cup all-purpose flour
- 1 teaspoon baking powder
- 1/4 teaspoon salt
- 1 cup milk
- 1 large egg
- 1 cup mushrooms, sliced
- 1 teaspoon fresh thyme (or 1/2 teaspoon dried thyme)
- Oil or butter for frying

Instructions:

1. In a bowl, mix flour, baking powder, and salt.
2. In another bowl, whisk together milk and egg.
3. Combine wet and dry ingredients until just mixed.
4. Sauté mushrooms in oil or butter until tender, then fold into the batter along with thyme.
5. Heat oil or butter in a skillet over medium heat.
6. Pour batter onto the skillet and cook until golden brown on both sides.

Apple Cinnamon Pancakes

Ingredients:

- 1 cup all-purpose flour
- 1 tablespoon sugar
- 1 teaspoon baking powder
- 1/2 teaspoon baking soda
- 1/4 teaspoon salt
- 1 cup buttermilk
- 1 large egg
- 1 apple, peeled and diced
- 1 teaspoon cinnamon
- Maple syrup for serving
- Butter for frying

Instructions:

1. In a bowl, mix flour, sugar, baking powder, baking soda, salt, and cinnamon.
2. In another bowl, whisk together buttermilk and egg.
3. Combine wet and dry ingredients until just mixed, then fold in diced apple.
4. Heat butter in a skillet over medium heat.
5. Pour batter onto the skillet and cook until bubbles form, then flip and cook until golden brown.
6. Serve with maple syrup.

Bacon and Cheddar Pancakes

Ingredients:

- 1 cup all-purpose flour
- 1 teaspoon baking powder
- 1/4 teaspoon salt
- 1 cup milk
- 1 large egg
- 1/2 cup cooked bacon, crumbled
- 1/2 cup cheddar cheese, shredded
- Oil or butter for frying

Instructions:

1. In a bowl, mix flour, baking powder, and salt.
2. In another bowl, whisk together milk and egg.
3. Combine wet and dry ingredients until just mixed, then fold in crumbled bacon and cheddar cheese.
4. Heat oil or butter in a skillet over medium heat.
5. Pour batter onto the skillet and cook until golden brown on both sides.

Raspberry Lemonade Pancakes

Ingredients:

- 1 cup all-purpose flour
- 2 tablespoons sugar
- 1 teaspoon baking powder
- 1/2 teaspoon baking soda
- 1/4 teaspoon salt
- 1 cup lemonade
- 1 large egg
- 1/2 cup raspberries (fresh or frozen)
- Oil or butter for frying

Instructions:

1. In a bowl, mix flour, sugar, baking powder, baking soda, and salt.
2. In another bowl, whisk together lemonade and egg.
3. Combine wet and dry ingredients until just mixed, then fold in raspberries.
4. Heat oil or butter in a skillet over medium heat.
5. Pour batter onto the skillet and cook until bubbles form, then flip and cook until golden brown.

Savory Carrot and Onion Pancakes

Ingredients:

- 1 cup all-purpose flour
- 1 teaspoon baking powder
- 1/2 teaspoon salt
- 1 cup milk
- 1 large egg
- 1 cup grated carrots
- 1/2 cup onion, finely chopped
- Oil or butter for frying

Instructions:

1. In a bowl, mix flour, baking powder, and salt.
2. In another bowl, whisk together milk and egg.
3. Combine wet and dry ingredients until just mixed, then fold in grated carrots and chopped onion.
4. Heat oil or butter in a skillet over medium heat.
5. Pour batter onto the skillet and cook until golden brown on both sides.

Chocolate Banana Pancakes

Ingredients:

- 1 cup all-purpose flour
- 2 tablespoons sugar
- 1 teaspoon baking powder
- 1/2 teaspoon baking soda
- 1/4 teaspoon salt
- 1 cup milk
- 1 large egg
- 1 ripe banana, mashed
- 1/4 cup chocolate chips
- Oil or butter for frying

Instructions:

1. In a bowl, mix flour, sugar, baking powder, baking soda, and salt.
2. In another bowl, whisk together milk, egg, and mashed banana.
3. Combine wet and dry ingredients until just mixed, then fold in chocolate chips.
4. Heat oil or butter in a skillet over medium heat.
5. Pour batter onto the skillet and cook until bubbles form, then flip and cook until golden brown.

Tomato and Basil Pancakes

Ingredients:

- 1 cup all-purpose flour
- 1 teaspoon baking powder
- 1/4 teaspoon salt
- 1 cup milk
- 1 large egg
- 1 cup cherry tomatoes, halved
- 1/4 cup fresh basil, chopped
- Oil or butter for frying

Instructions:

1. In a bowl, mix flour, baking powder, and salt.
2. In another bowl, whisk together milk and egg.
3. Combine wet and dry ingredients until just mixed, then fold in cherry tomatoes and chopped basil.
4. Heat oil or butter in a skillet over medium heat.
5. Pour batter onto the skillet and cook until golden brown on both sides.

Blackberry Sage Pancakes

Ingredients:

- 1 cup all-purpose flour
- 2 tablespoons sugar
- 1 teaspoon baking powder
- 1/2 teaspoon baking soda
- 1/4 teaspoon salt
- 1 cup buttermilk
- 1 large egg
- 1/2 cup blackberries, halved
- 1 teaspoon fresh sage, chopped
- Butter for frying

Instructions:

1. In a bowl, mix flour, sugar, baking powder, baking soda, and salt.
2. In another bowl, whisk together buttermilk and egg.
3. Combine wet and dry ingredients until just mixed, then fold in blackberries and sage.
4. Heat butter in a skillet over medium heat.
5. Pour batter onto the skillet and cook until bubbles form, then flip and cook until golden brown.

Savory Beetroot Pancakes

Ingredients:

- 1 cup all-purpose flour
- 1 teaspoon baking powder
- 1/4 teaspoon salt
- 1 cup milk
- 1 large egg
- 1 cup cooked beetroot, pureed
- 1 tablespoon fresh dill, chopped
- Oil or butter for frying

Instructions:

1. In a bowl, mix flour, baking powder, and salt.
2. In another bowl, whisk together milk, egg, and beetroot puree.
3. Combine wet and dry ingredients until just mixed, then fold in dill.
4. Heat oil or butter in a skillet over medium heat.
5. Pour batter onto the skillet and cook until golden brown on both sides.

Honey Lavender Pancakes

Ingredients:

- 1 cup all-purpose flour
- 2 tablespoons sugar
- 1 teaspoon baking powder
- 1/2 teaspoon baking soda
- 1/4 teaspoon salt
- 1 cup buttermilk
- 1 large egg
- 1 tablespoon dried culinary lavender
- 2 tablespoons honey
- Butter for frying

Instructions:

1. In a bowl, mix flour, sugar, baking powder, baking soda, and salt.
2. In another bowl, whisk together buttermilk, egg, honey, and lavender.
3. Combine wet and dry ingredients until just mixed.
4. Heat butter in a skillet over medium heat.
5. Pour batter onto the skillet and cook until bubbles form, then flip and cook until golden brown.

Jalapeño Cornbread Pancakes

Ingredients:

- 1 cup cornmeal
- 1/2 cup all-purpose flour
- 1 tablespoon sugar
- 1 teaspoon baking powder
- 1/2 teaspoon baking soda
- 1/4 teaspoon salt
- 1 cup buttermilk
- 1 large egg
- 1 jalapeño, finely chopped
- Butter for frying

Instructions:

1. In a bowl, mix cornmeal, flour, sugar, baking powder, baking soda, and salt.
2. In another bowl, whisk together buttermilk, egg, and jalapeño.
3. Combine wet and dry ingredients until just mixed.
4. Heat butter in a skillet over medium heat.
5. Pour batter onto the skillet and cook until golden brown on both sides.

Coconut Lime Pancakes

Ingredients:

- 1 cup all-purpose flour
- 2 tablespoons sugar
- 1 teaspoon baking powder
- 1/2 teaspoon baking soda
- 1/4 teaspoon salt
- 1 cup coconut milk
- 1 large egg
- Zest and juice of 1 lime
- 1/4 cup shredded coconut
- Butter for frying

Instructions:

1. In a bowl, mix flour, sugar, baking powder, baking soda, and salt.
2. In another bowl, whisk together coconut milk, egg, lime zest, lime juice, and shredded coconut.
3. Combine wet and dry ingredients until just mixed.
4. Heat butter in a skillet over medium heat.
5. Pour batter onto the skillet and cook until bubbles form, then flip and cook until golden brown.

Feta and Spinach Pancakes

Ingredients:

- 1 cup all-purpose flour
- 1 teaspoon baking powder
- 1/4 teaspoon salt
- 1 cup milk
- 1 large egg
- 1 cup fresh spinach, chopped
- 1/2 cup feta cheese, crumbled
- Oil or butter for frying

Instructions:

1. In a bowl, mix flour, baking powder, and salt.
2. In another bowl, whisk together milk and egg.
3. Combine wet and dry ingredients until just mixed, then fold in spinach and feta cheese.
4. Heat oil or butter in a skillet over medium heat.
5. Pour batter onto the skillet and cook until golden brown on both sides.

Chocolate Mint Pancakes

Ingredients:

- 1 cup all-purpose flour
- 2 tablespoons sugar
- 1 teaspoon baking powder
- 1/2 teaspoon baking soda
- 1/4 teaspoon salt
- 1 cup buttermilk
- 1 large egg
- 1/4 cup cocoa powder
- 1 teaspoon peppermint extract
- Butter for frying

Instructions:

1. In a bowl, mix flour, sugar, baking powder, baking soda, salt, and cocoa powder.
2. In another bowl, whisk together buttermilk, egg, and peppermint extract.
3. Combine wet and dry ingredients until just mixed.
4. Heat butter in a skillet over medium heat.
5. Pour batter onto the skillet and cook until bubbles form, then flip and cook until golden brown.

Corn and Zucchini Pancakes

Ingredients:

- 1 cup all-purpose flour
- 1 teaspoon baking powder
- 1/4 teaspoon salt
- 1 cup milk
- 1 large egg
- 1 cup corn kernels (fresh or frozen)
- 1 cup zucchini, grated
- Oil or butter for frying

Instructions:

1. In a bowl, mix flour, baking powder, and salt.
2. In another bowl, whisk together milk and egg.
3. Combine wet and dry ingredients until just mixed, then fold in corn and zucchini.
4. Heat oil or butter in a skillet over medium heat.
5. Pour batter onto the skillet and cook until golden brown on both sides.

Blackberry Coconut Pancakes

Ingredients:

- 1 cup all-purpose flour
- 2 tablespoons sugar
- 1 teaspoon baking powder
- 1/2 teaspoon baking soda
- 1/4 teaspoon salt
- 1 cup coconut milk
- 1 large egg
- 1/2 cup blackberries, halved
- 1/4 cup shredded coconut
- Butter for frying

Instructions:

1. In a bowl, mix flour, sugar, baking powder, baking soda, and salt.
2. In another bowl, whisk together coconut milk and egg.
3. Combine wet and dry ingredients until just mixed, then fold in blackberries and shredded coconut.
4. Heat butter in a skillet over medium heat.
5. Pour batter onto the skillet and cook until bubbles form, then flip and cook until golden brown.

Herb and Parmesan Pancakes

Ingredients:

- 1 cup all-purpose flour
- 1 teaspoon baking powder
- 1/2 teaspoon salt
- 1 cup milk
- 1 large egg
- 1/2 cup grated Parmesan cheese
- 1 tablespoon fresh herbs (such as parsley or chives), chopped
- Butter for frying

Instructions:

1. In a bowl, mix flour, baking powder, and salt.
2. In another bowl, whisk together milk and egg.
3. Combine wet and dry ingredients until just mixed, then fold in Parmesan and herbs.
4. Heat butter in a skillet over medium heat.
5. Pour batter onto the skillet and cook until golden brown on both sides.

Honey Almond Pancakes

Ingredients:

- 1 cup all-purpose flour
- 2 tablespoons sugar
- 1 teaspoon baking powder
- 1/2 teaspoon baking soda
- 1/4 teaspoon salt
- 1 cup milk
- 1 large egg
- 1/4 cup almond butter
- 2 tablespoons honey
- Sliced almonds for topping

Instructions:

1. In a bowl, mix flour, sugar, baking powder, baking soda, and salt.
2. In another bowl, whisk together milk, egg, almond butter, and honey.
3. Combine wet and dry ingredients until just mixed.
4. Heat butter in a skillet over medium heat.
5. Pour batter onto the skillet and cook until golden brown on both sides. Top with sliced almonds.

Savory Egg and Cheese Pancakes

Ingredients:

- 1 cup all-purpose flour
- 1 teaspoon baking powder
- 1/4 teaspoon salt
- 1 cup milk
- 1 large egg
- 1/2 cup shredded cheese (cheddar or your choice)
- 2 large eggs (for cooking)
- Butter for frying

Instructions:

1. In a bowl, mix flour, baking powder, and salt.
2. In another bowl, whisk together milk and egg.
3. Combine wet and dry ingredients until just mixed, then fold in shredded cheese.
4. Heat butter in a skillet over medium heat.
5. Pour batter onto the skillet and cook until golden brown on both sides. In a separate pan, cook two eggs sunny-side up. Serve pancakes topped with eggs.

Churro Pancakes

Ingredients:

- 1 cup all-purpose flour
- 2 tablespoons sugar
- 1 teaspoon baking powder
- 1/2 teaspoon baking soda
- 1/4 teaspoon salt
- 1 cup milk
- 1 large egg
- 1 teaspoon cinnamon
- Butter for frying
- Sugar and cinnamon mixture for topping

Instructions:

1. In a bowl, mix flour, sugar, baking powder, baking soda, salt, and cinnamon.
2. In another bowl, whisk together milk and egg.
3. Combine wet and dry ingredients until just mixed.
4. Heat butter in a skillet over medium heat.
5. Pour batter onto the skillet and cook until golden brown on both sides.
6. Toss pancakes in the sugar and cinnamon mixture before serving.

Savory Quinoa and Spinach Pancakes

Ingredients:

- 1 cup cooked quinoa
- 1/2 cup all-purpose flour
- 1 teaspoon baking powder
- 1/4 teaspoon salt
- 1 cup milk
- 1 large egg
- 1 cup fresh spinach, chopped
- Oil or butter for frying

Instructions:

1. In a bowl, mix quinoa, flour, baking powder, and salt.
2. In another bowl, whisk together milk and egg.
3. Combine wet and dry ingredients until just mixed, then fold in spinach.
4. Heat oil or butter in a skillet over medium heat.
5. Pour batter onto the skillet and cook until golden brown on both sides.

Maple Pecan Pancakes

Ingredients:

- 1 cup all-purpose flour
- 2 tablespoons sugar
- 1 teaspoon baking powder
- 1/2 teaspoon baking soda
- 1/4 teaspoon salt
- 1 cup buttermilk
- 1 large egg
- 1/2 cup chopped pecans
- Maple syrup for serving

Instructions:

1. In a bowl, mix flour, sugar, baking powder, baking soda, and salt.
2. In another bowl, whisk together buttermilk and egg.
3. Combine wet and dry ingredients until just mixed, then fold in chopped pecans.
4. Heat butter in a skillet over medium heat.
5. Pour batter onto the skillet and cook until golden brown on both sides. Serve with maple syrup.

Sweet and Savory Vegetable Pancakes

Ingredients:

- 1 cup all-purpose flour
- 1 teaspoon baking powder
- 1/2 teaspoon salt
- 1 cup milk
- 1 large egg
- 1/2 cup grated vegetables (zucchini, carrots, or squash)
- 1 tablespoon honey or maple syrup
- Oil or butter for frying

Instructions:

1. In a bowl, mix flour, baking powder, and salt.
2. In another bowl, whisk together milk, egg, and honey or maple syrup.
3. Combine wet and dry ingredients until just mixed, then fold in grated vegetables.
4. Heat oil or butter in a skillet over medium heat.
5. Pour batter onto the skillet and cook until golden brown on both sides.